NATIVE WISDOM

D0668264

NATIVE WISDOM

Edited by

JOSEPH BRUCHAC

HarperSanFrancisco
A Division of HarperCollins*Publishers*

HarperSanFrancisco and the author, in association with The Basic Foundation, a not-for-profit organization whose primary mission is reforestation, will facilitate the planting of two trees for every one tree used in the manufacture of this book.

All texts reprinted by permission. Acknowledgments begin in the notes, page 95.

NATIVE WISDOM. Copyright © 1995 by Joseph Bruchac. All rights reserved. Printed in the United States of America. No part of this book may be used or reproduced in any manner whatsoever without written permission except in the case of brief quotations embodied in critical articles and reviews. For information address HarperCollins Publishers, 10 East 53rd Street, New York, NY 10022.

Book design by Jaime Robles

Library of Congress Cataloging-in-Publication Data
Native wisdom/edited by Joseph Bruchac. — 1st ed.
p.   cm.
Includes bibliographical references.
ISBN 0–06–251172–6 (pbk. : alk. paper)
1. Indian philosophy—North America. 2. Indians of North America—
Quotations. 3. Speeches, addresses, etc., Indian—North America.
4. Indian poetry—North America. I. Bruchac, Joseph
E98.P5N383 1995
191'.089'97—dc20   94–29472

95   96   97   98   99   ❖ HAD   10   9   8   7   6   5   4   3   2

This edition is printed on acid-free paper that meets the American
National Standards Institute Z39.48 Standard.

contents

MANY ROADS LEAD TO THE HEART
OF THE LAND:
An Introduction 1

THE EAST 7

THE SOUTH 23

THE WEST 31

THE NORTH 43

THE SKY ABOVE 51

THE EARTH BELOW 59

THE SACRED PLACE WITHIN 67

THE CIRCLE 81

NOTES 95

To my teachers.
Wzawmi Ogahkimaw.

You look at me and you see only an ugly old man, but within I am filled with great beauty. I sit as on a mountaintop and look into the future. I see my people and your people living together. In time to come my people will have forgotten their early way of life unless they learn it from white men's books. So you must write down what I tell you; and you must have it made into a book that coming generations may know this truth.

SANDOVAL, HASTIN TLO'TSI HEE/
OLD MAN BUFFALO GRASS (Navajo), 1928[1]

o I know that it is a good thing I am going to do; and because no good thing can be done by any man alone, I will first make an offering and send a voice to the spirit of the world, that it may help me to be true. See I fill this sacred pipe with the bark of the red willow; but before we smoke it you must see how it is made and what it means. These four ribbons hanging here on the stem are the four quarters of the universe. The black one is for the west where the thunder beings live to send us rain; the white one for the north, whence comes the great white cleansing wind; the red one for the east, whence springs the light and where the morning star lives to give men wisdom; the yellow for the south, whence comes the summer and the power to grow.

BLACK ELK
(Oglala Lakota), 1931[2]

I can tell you right now,
there are no secrets.
There's no mystery.
There's only common sense.

OREN LYONS,
**Faithkeeper of the Turtle Clan
(Onondaga), 1990[3]**

The more you know
The more you will trust
and the less you will fear

MEDEWIWIN PRAYER (Ojibway)

MANY ROADS LEAD TO THE HEART OF THE LAND: AN INTRODUCTION

Although the words in this book represent some of the most powerful words of wisdom offered by the Native peoples of North America, this book must be seen as no more than what it is—a part of a much greater whole. The circle outside this book, the natural world and the words of the elders, is a much greater circle, and, though shaken by the carelessness of the modern world, it goes on unbroken.

A book of wisdom such as this could have been put together from any one of the many American Indian nations. I have chosen to draw from many to give a sense of the diversity and the common themes in Native American wisdom, a wisdom I firmly believe is greatly needed today—by all human beings.

Remember, too, that wise words can have more than one meaning, more than one use. Black Elk, one of the most famous of Native America's spiritual teachers, in telling his life story *Black Elk Speaks* had also a very Lakota purpose, the survival of his own people. So, though I have chosen selections with clear and understandable meanings on the surface, it should be recognized that many of these excerpts have been translated from an original language in which additional meanings reside. Even in English they may hold other levels of meaning understandable only to those who have learned enough. Of course, many levels of meaning can be found in such sacred texts as the Bible, the Koran, and the Upanishads, but people often forget that Native American wisdom has the same depth as other spiritual teachings.

The cosmos of the Native North American was, and to a large degree still is, a universe shaped by and viewed through the spirit. Certain women and men of the hundreds of different

American Indian nations have always answered the calling to be medicine people, priests, healers, doctors, and shamans—specialists in the realm of the sacred. Yet people of the nations have always understood that every human being can have direct access to that spiritual realm and that no intermediary is ever needed to be able to gain wisdom or to pray.

Moreover, the presence of the spirit of creation, an indescribable and awesome force called Orenda by the Iroquois and Wakan by the Lakota, is not just concentrated in special holy places, shrines, and ritual objects that symbolize the spirit. The "Great Mystery," Ktsinwaskw to the Abenaki people, is also in and of all things. As Black Elk said, "Everywhere is the center of the world." Everything is sacred.

One of my favorite stories—a story I learned from Kevin Locke, a contemporary Lakota storyteller—is of the Seventh Direction. After Wakan Tanka, the Great Spirit, arranged the other six directions—East, South, West, North, Above, and

Below—one direction was still left to be placed. But since that Seventh Direction was the most powerful of all, the one containing the greatest wisdom and strength, Wakan Tanka, the Great Spirit, wished to place it somewhere where it would not easily be found. So it was finally hidden in the last place humans usually think to look—in each person's heart. A personal relationship to the Creator, the Great Spirit, is in Native American cultures not something that must be created. It is something that must be remembered.

It is important to understand that there are many different ways of seeing the world and expressing the wisdom of Native beliefs among the more than four hundred different original nations of North America. No one Native voice speaks for all voices, though some things are largely held in common, among them the belief that health (spiritual and physical) is natural and connected to living and walking in balance.

Many roads lead to the heart. This book is like a road map that helps you see the destination, if only from a distance. If you know how to read the map, you can follow the roads into the land that you seek.

NOTE: One of the most famous pieces of Native American wisdom, the speech of Chief Seathl, is *not* included in its entirety in this book but is represented only by a relatively brief quotation from the original published text. The words that Seathl spoke, sometime around December 1854, were probably spoken in Lutshootseed, translated into the very limited Chinook trade jargon, then translated into English. Dr. Henry Smith took notes from that English translation to write his version of the speech, doing so in a flowery Victorian style that has as much of Smith in it as of Seathl. To be fair to Smith, he visited Seathl many times afterward, trying to make his version of the speech convey the meaning Seathl intended. However, some of the currently most famous parts of what is supposed to be Seathl's speech were added in the twentieth century by non-Indian speech writers. At present, elders of the Suquamish and Duwamish Nation are putting together their own version of the speech that their traditions indicate Seathl actually gave.

chapter one

THE EAST

The start of life's journey, the new day, is in the East. Just as it is the place on this continent where the European world first came into contact with the Native people of North America, it is the place of beginnings, first light—and the possibility of starting again.

WABANAKI

*T*hese days people seek knowledge, not wisdom. Knowledge is of the past; wisdom is of the future.

VERNON COOPER (Lumbee), 1990[4]

This chant is part of a healing ceremony incorporating sand painting, singing, and the gathering of a large number of people who lend support to the healing of the person who is ill. Among the Navajo, health is regarded as natural and sickness is a result of imbalance. Thus the ceremony restores balance to the person who is ill. The Navajo word hozhoni, *which is translated here as "beauty" or "happily," combines the concepts of beauty, peace, harmony, and happiness.*

The House Made of Dawn,
from *The Night Chant*

In Tsegihi,
In the house made of dawn,
In the house made of evening twilight,
In the house made of dark cloud,
In the house made of male rain,
In the house made of dark mist,
In the house made of female rain,
In the house made of pollen,
In the house made of grasshoppers,
Where the dark mist curtains the doorway,
The path to which is on the rainbow,
Where the zig-zag lightning stands on top,
Where the he-rain stands high on top,
Oh, male divinity!
With your moccasins of dark cloud, come to us.
With your leggings of dark cloud, come to us.
With your shirt of dark cloud, come to us.
With your headdress of dark cloud,
        come to us.

With your mind enveloped in dark cloud,
    come to us.
With the dark thunder above you, come to us
    soaring.
With the shapen cloud at your feet, come to us
    soaring.
With the far darkness made of the dark cloud
    over your head, come to us soaring.
With the far darkness made of the male rain
    over your head, come to us soaring.
With the far darkness made of the female rain
    over your head, come to us soaring.
With the zig-zag lightning flung out on high
    over your head, come to us soaring.
With the rainbow hanging high
    over your head, come to us soaring.
With the far darkness made of the dark cloud
    on the ends of your wings, come to us
        soaring.
With the darkness on the earth, come to us.
I have made your sacrifice.
I have prepared a smoke for you.

My feet restore for me.
My limbs restore for me.
My body restore for me.
My mind restore for me.
My voice restore for me.
Today, take out your spell for me.
Today, take away your spell for me.
Away from me you have taken it.
Far off from me it is taken.
Far off you have done it.
Happily I recover.
Happily my interior grows cool.
Happily my limbs regain their power.
Happily my head becomes cool.
Happily I hear again.
Happily I walk.
Impervious to pain, I walk.
Feeling light within, I walk.
With lively feelings, I walk. . . .

Happily the old men will regard you.
Happily the old women will regard you.

Happily the young men will regard you.
Happily the young women will regard you.
Happily the boys will regard you.
Happily the girls will regard you.
Happily the children will regard you.
Happily the chiefs will regard you.
Happily, as they scatter in different directions,
     they will regard you.
Happily, as they approach their homes,
     they will regard you.
Happily may their roads home be on the trail of
     pollen.
Happily may they all get back.
In beauty I walk.
With beauty before me, I walk.
With beauty behind me, I walk.
With beauty below me, I walk.
With beauty above me, I walk.
With beauty all around me, I walk.
It is finished in beauty.
It is finished in beauty.

TRADITIONAL (Navajo), translated in 1897⁵

From the beginning there were drums, beating out world rhythm—the booming, never-failing tide on the beach; the four seasons, gliding smoothly, one from the other; when the birds come, when they go, the bear hibernating for his winter sleep. Unfathomable the why, yet all in perfect time.

Watch the heartbeat in your wrist—a precise pulsing beat of life's Drum—with loss of timing you are ill.

JIMALEE BURTON (Cherokee), 1974[6]

Being born as humans to this earth is a very sacred trust. We have a sacred responsibility because of the special gift we have, which is beyond the fine gifts of the plant life, the fish, the woodlands, the birds, and all the other living things on earth. We are able to take care of them.

AUDREY SHENANDOAH (Onondaga), 1987[7]

Our fathers gave us many laws, which they had learned from their fathers. Those laws were good. They told us to treat all men as they treated us, that we should never be the first to break a bargain, that it was a disgrace to tell a lie, that we should only speak the truth. . . .

CHIEF JOSEPH (Nez Perce), 1879[8]

Everything that gives birth is female. When men begin to understand the relationships of the universe that women have always known, the world will begin to change for the better.

LORRAINE CANOE (Mohawk), 1993[9]

Why will you take from us by force what you can obtain by love? Why will you destroy us who you supply with food? What can you get by war? We are unarmed, and willing to give you what you ask, if you come in a friendly manner. . . .

I am not so simple as to not know it is better to eat good meat, sleep comfortably, live quietly with my women and children, laugh and be merry with the English, and being their friend, trade for their copper and hatchets, than to run away from them. . . .

Take away your guns and swords, the cause of all our jealousy, or you may die in the same manner.

WAHUNSONACOCK [Powhatan]
(Powhatan Confederacy), 1609[10]

Spoken in the 17th Century to Baron De Lahontan, Lord Lieutenant of the French Colony at Placentia in Newfoundland

In earnest, my dear Brother, I am sorry for you from the bottom of my soul. Take my advice, and turn HURON; for I see plainly a vast difference between your condition and mine. I am master of my condition and mine. I have the absolute disposal of my self, I do what I please, I am the first and the last of my nation, I fear no man and I depend only on the Great Spirit. Whereas, your body, as well as your soul, are doomed to a dependence upon your great captain, your Viceroy disposes of you, you have not the liberty of doing what you have a mind to, you are afraid of robbers, false witnesses and assassins and you depend upon an infinity of persons whose places have raised them above you. Is it true or not?

KONDIARONK (Huron), circa 1690[11]

Spoken in 1676 by a Micmac Chief in Nova Scotia

It is true we have not always had the use of bread and of wine which your France produces; but, in fact, before the arrival of the French in these parts, did not the Micmac live much longer than now? If we have not any longer among us any of those old men of a hundred and thirty to forty years, it is only because we are gradually adopting your manner of living, for experience is making it very plain that those of us live longest who, despising your bread, your wine, and your brandy, are content with their natural food of beaver, of moose, of waterfowl and fish, in accord with the custom of our ancestors and of all the Micmac nation. Learn now, my brother, once for all, because I must open to you my heart, there is no Indian who does not consider himself infinitely more happy and more powerful than the French.

ANONYMOUS (Micmac), 1676[12]

I see another sun
because Mu'ndu
is good
exceedingly.

I know Mu'ndu.

Humans make but little.
They think they know much.

All things declare
Mu'ndu had made them.

I cannot make myself,
they declare.
Humans cannot make one tree.

Ni ya'yo.
That is so.

FIDELIA FIELDING/
FLYING BIRD (Mohegan),
diary entry for June 9, 1904[13]

Sections from *The Law of the Great Peace*

Regarded as the world's oldest living constitution, the five nations of the Iroquois made an agreement among their nations sometime around 1390. In forming the league out of five previously warring though related nations, the Iroquois planted a symbolic tree of peace. Contemporary United States symbols borrowed from the imagery of the Tree of Peace and the united league of the Iroquois include the eagle clutching arrows bound together, which appears on the back of the quarter. These sections are taken from the version of The Law of the Great Peace *authorized by the contemporary Iroquois League of Six Nations.*

2.

Roots have spread out from the Tree of Great Peace, one to the north, one to the east, one to the south, and one to the west. These are the

Great White Roots and their nature is Peace and Strength.

If any man or any nation of the Five Nations shall obey the laws of the Great Peace (Kaianerekowa) and shall make this known to the statesmen of the League, they may trace back the roots to the Tree. If their minds are clean, and if they are obedient and promise to obey the wishes of the Council of the League, they shall be welcomed to take shelter beneath the Great Evergreen Tree.

We place at the top of the Tree of Great Peace an eagle, who is able to see afar. If he sees in the distance any danger threatening, he will at once warn the people of the League.

24.

The chiefs of the League of Five Nations shall be the mentors of the people for all time. The thickness of their skin shall be seven spans (tsiataniiorionkarake), which is to say that they shall be proof against anger, offensive action, and criticism. Their hearts shall be full of peace and good will, and their minds filled with a yearning for the welfare of the people of the League. With endless patience, they shall carry out their duty. Their firmness shall be tempered with a tenderness for the people. Neither anger nor fury shall find lodging in their minds, and all their actions shall be marked by calm deliberation.

57.

Five arrows shall be bound together very strong and shall represent one Nation each. As the five arrows are strongly bound, this shall symbolize the complete union of the nations. Thus are the Five Nations completely united and enfolded together, united into one head, one body, and one mind. They shall labor, legislate and council together for the interest of future generations.

TRADITIONAL (Iroquois), circa 1390[14]

chapter TWO

THE SOUTH

The South holds the warmth of summer. It is a time of innocence, of learning and growth.

CHITIMACHA

From the Zuni Ceremony Done on the Eighth Day of an Infant's Life

Now this is the day
Our child
Into the daylight
You will go out standing
Preparing for your days.
When all your days were at an end,
When eight days were past,
Our sun father
Went in to sit down at his sacred place.
And our night fathers
Having come out standing to their sacred place,
Passing a blessed night
We came to day.
Now this day
Our fathers,
Dawn priests,
Have come out standing to their sacred place.
Our sun father
Has come out standing to his sacred place,

Our child,
It is your day.
This day,
The flesh of the white corn,
Prayer meal,
To our sun father
This prayer meal we offer.
May your road be fulfilled
reaching to the road of your sun father.
When your road is fulfilled
In your thoughts
May we be the ones whom your thoughts will
        embrace,
For this, on this day
To our sun father
We offer prayer meal
To this end
May you help us all to finish our roads.

TRADITIONAL (Zuni), translated in 1939[15]

The earth hears you
the sky and wood mountain see you.
If you will believe this,
you will grow old.

ANONYMOUS (Luiseno)[16]

All through this time I never asked of them (grand-
mother and grandfather) or anyone, "why?" It
would have meant that I was learning nothing—
that I was stupid. And in Western Society if you
don't ask why they think you are stupid. So, hav-
ing been raised to not ask why but to listen, be-
come aware, I take for granted that people have
some knowledge of themselves and myself—that
is religion. Then when we know ourselves we can
put our feelings together and share this knowledge.

SOGE TRACK (Taos Pueblo), 1976[17]

Training began with children who were taught to
sit still and enjoy it. They were taught to use their
organs of smell, to look when there was appar-

ently nothing to see, and to listen intently when all seemingly was quiet. A child that cannot sit still is a half-developed child.

CHIEF LUTHER STANDING BEAR
(Lakota), 1936[18]

You don't ask questions when you grow up. You watch and listen and wait, and the answer will come to you.

LARRY BIRD (Laguna Pueblo)[19]

Talk slowly and kindly to children.
Never punish them unjustly.

If a child does not obey,
let the mother say,
"Come to the water
and I will dunk you."
And if the child
still does not obey
let her say this again.

If at the third time
obedience still has not come
then the child should be dunked
in the water.

But if the child cries for mercy
that child must have mercy.

So they said and he said.
It was that way.
Eniaehuk.

HANDSOME LAKE (Seneca),
circa 1800[20]

A Mother's Advice

Live a quiet life and be kind to all, especially the old, and listen to the advice of the old. People will respect you if you do this and be kind to you. Do not run after a boy. If a young man wants to marry you, let him come here to see you and come here to live with you. This is the reason I am always telling you to be industrious and how to live, so

when you have a home you will be industrious
and do right to the people around you.

NODINENS (Chippewa), 1929[21]

My children, as you travel along life's road never
harm anyone, nor cause anyone to feel sad. On the
contrary, if at any time you can make a person
happy, do.

ANONYMOUS (Winnebago), circa 1923[22]

My people were wise. They never neglected the
young or failed to keep before them deeds done by
illustrious men of the tribe. Our teachers were
willing and thorough. They were our grandfathers,
fathers, or uncles. All were quick to praise excellence without speaking a word that might break
the spirit of a boy who might be less capable than
others. The boy who failed at any lesson got only
more lessons, more care, until he was as far as he
could go.

PLENTY-COUPS (Crow), 1928[23]

In our way of life, in our government, with every decision we make, we always keep in mind the Seventh Generation to come. It's our job to see that the people coming ahead, the generations still unborn, have a world no worse than ours—and hopefully better. When we walk upon Mother Earth we always plant our feet carefully because we know the faces of our future generations are looking up at us from beneath the ground. We never forget them.

 OREN LYONS (Onondaga), 1990[24]

In every human heart there is a deep spiritual hunger for an abiding, steadfast faith, a positive, satisfying belief in some future existence. Such a faith stabilizes character, and many of our young people have no such anchor for their souls.

THOMAS WILDCAT ALFORD (Shawnee), 1930[25]

chapter three

THE WEST

The West reminds us of the wisdom of maturity with the approach of the sunset. It is the time of parenthood, responsibility, and good sense—the time to teach, acknowledge, and give thanks.

ACOMA

We are the Original People of the Western Hemisphere, people who have been on this part of the world for thousands and thousands of years. No man has ever set the time and ever set the date of how we originated in this part of the world. Our history dates back according to our traditions to the beginning of time.

At the beginning of time, at the time of Creation, also our people came about. We had no teachers, we had no instructors, we had no schools. We had to turn and look at the Creation. We had to study Nature. And we had to copy off of Nature. Our entire civilization was built upon the study of Nature. They became our instructors in the beginning of times. Our religion was found at this time. Our way of life we founded through that type of study.

So we organized our governments under the study of Nature. We lived under an unchanging government, a traditional government of our ancestors. That law that we lived by never changed until recent years. In 1492 that law of our ancestors began to change.

A government that is thousands of years old is what we lived by. That law was workable for us. We lived by understood laws. Today all over our country historians, anthropology people, have dug up the earth to find the history of the Western hemisphere. But they have not found any jail house. They have not found any prisons. They have not found insane asylums. How did different nations of people speaking so many different languages live without those institutions? Time came when that law with that government was interrupted. Prior to 1492 we lived a life. That life was valuable for us.

That religion was understood by all Native people of the Western hemisphere. Time came when we were told that the religion is not the right one, therefore it has never been recognized until this day by the world. We were forced to accept the recognized religion. Many of our people were

Christianized and left the ancient religion of their ancestors.

We still look at Nature and watch how they grow little ones. We find the ducks, we find the geese still yet living with that thousand-year old government. The animals, they still continue to follow that government that was given to them at the beginning of time. Original instructions of life were given at the beginning of time to all living things.

The entire Creation still follows those Instructions of Life. The tree, the fruits, they never fail. They never make a mistake to bring their fruits in their season. The animals never make a mistake. They still live as they were created. Among the Creation, what is Man's Instructions of Life? We see the Creation ... Life, the circle, a measurement with no beginning and no ending.

PHILLIP DEERE (Muskogee-Creek), 1977[26]

It is going to be the job of Native women to begin teaching other women what their roles are.

Women have to turn life around, because if they don't, all of future life is threatened and endangered. I don't care what kind of women they are, they are going to have to worry more about the changes that are taking place on this Mother Earth that will affect us all.

YET SI BLUE/JANET MCCLOUD
(Tulalip), 1993[27]

There are four ways in which you may go, if you are going somewhere. The first is to go immediately on first thought. That is not right. Think about it. This will make it the second way. Then think about it a third time, but don't go yet. Then on the fourth consideration, go and it will be all right. Thus you will be safe. Sometimes wait a day in between consideration of your problems.

DIABLO (White Mountain Apache), 1942[28]

Woman's Prayer When Gathering Roots from a Young Cedar Tree

Look at me, friend!
I have come to ask
for your dress,
for you have come
to take pity on us;
for there is nothing
for which you cannot be used,
because it is your way
that there is nothing
for which we cannot use you,
for you are really willing
to give us your dress.
I have come to beg you,
for this, long life–maker,
for I am going to make
a basket for lily roots out of you.

TRADITIONAL (Kwakiutl), 1921[29]

No talk is ever given without first indicating your humility. "I am an ignorant man; I am a poor man"—all the talks start this way—"I don't know nearly as much as you men sitting around here, but I would like to offer my humble opinion," and then he'll knock you down with logic and wisdom.

ALLEN C. QUETONE (Kiowa), 1974[30]

The Indian has more sense than the white man. The duellist may possess some *physical* bravery, but he lacks the moral courage of the Indian, who, when he was challenged, replied, "I have two objections to this duel affair; the one is, lest I should hurt *you*, and the other is, lest you should hurt *me*. I do not see any good that it would do me to put a bullet through your body—I could not make any use of you when dead; but I could of a rabbit or a turkey. As to myself, I think it more wise to avoid than to put myself in the way of harm; I am under apprehension that you might hit me. That being the case, I think it advisable to keep my distance. If you want to try your pistols, take some object—a tree, or anything about my size; and if you hit that, send me word, and I shall acknowledge, that had I been there you might have hit me."

CHIEF KAHKEWAQUONABY/
PETER JONES (Ojibway), 1861[31]

God created this Indian country and it was like He spread out a big blanket. He put the Indians on it. They were created here in this country, truly and honestly, and that was the time this river started to run. Then God created fish in this river and put deer in these mountains and made laws through which has come the increase of fish and game. Then the Creator gave us Indians life; we awakened and as soon as we saw the game and fish we knew that they were made for us. For the women God made roots and berries to gather, and the Indians grew and multiplied as a people. When we were created we were given our ground to live on, and from that time these were our rights. This is all true. We had the fish before the missionaries came, before the white man came. We were put here by the Creator and these were our rights as far as my memory to my great-grandfather. This was the food on which we lived. My mother gathered berries; my father fished and killed the game. These words are mine and they are true. It matters not how long I live, I cannot change these thoughts. My strength is from the fish; my blood is from the fish, from the roots and the berries. The fish and the game are the essence of my life. I was not brought here from a foreign country and did not come here. I was put here by the Creator.

MENINOCK (Yakima), 1915[32]

In the old days, the woman was the teacher, so my mother and my grandmother were our teachers. If we did something out of the way, they'd say "Nobody does that." And we'd get smart and say "If nobody does that then I want to." But it wouldn't work out for us! You see they were very strict with us. I remember my grandmother saying: "Don't go through fire. You're going to get burned and there are other ways to go around it."

MARGARET HAWK (Oglala Sioux), 1991[33]

Grandparents' Advice:

TO MOTHERS AND FATHERS

If your children go among the neighbors and make a quarrel, don't you take their part. You must bring them home and make them behave themselves. Do not get into a quarrel with your neighbors because of the quarrels of children.

Teach the children what is right to do, and they will live that way and get on well in the world.

Keep from quarreling, live peaceably and do not say bad things about each other.

Obey your parents, take their advice, and respect them. If you live in that way while you are among your own people you will be respected when you go to a strange village.

TRADITIONAL (Chippewa), 1929[34]

Song of the Young War God

I have been to the end of the earth.
I have been to the end of the waters.
I have been to the end of the sky.
I have been to the end of the mountains.
I have found none that were not my friends.

TRADITIONAL (Navajo), translated in 1897[35]

If everyone did something for somebody else, there wouldn't be anyone in need in the whole world. Just help somebody. It's not that way now, but I think people are going to learn.

MARLENE RICKARD (Tuscarora), 1993[36]

hat is a man?
A man is nothing.
Without his family
He is of less importance
Than that bug
Crossing a trail.

ANONYMOUS (Pomo), 1944[37]

chapter four

THE NORTH

The North holds that hard, cleansing wisdom of the time of winter and white hair, the elder's breath through the sacred pipe, the grandparents who, on life's great circle, are closest to the little children.

POTOWATOMI

It is important that you learn the past and act accordingly, for that will assure us that we will always people the earth. I say this because our people who have gone before have said this.

IGNATIA BROKER (Ojibway), 1983[38]

The Creator ordained
that people should live
to an old age.

When a woman becomes old
she will be without strength
and unable to work.

It is wrong to be unkind
to our Grandmothers.

The Creator forbids
unkindness to the Old.
We, the Four Messengers, say this.

The Creator made it
to be this way.
An old woman shall be
as a child again
and her grandchildren
shall care for her.
For only because she is,
they are.

So they said and he said.
It was that way.

HANDSOME LAKE
(Seneca), circa 1800[39]

What is life?
It is the flash
of a firefly in the night.

It is the breath
of a buffalo in the winter time.

It is the little shadow
which runs across the grass
and loses itself in the sunset.

CROWFOOT (Blackfeet), circa 1880⁴⁰

Old age is not as honorable as death,
but most people want it.

TWO LEGGINGS (Crow), 1919⁴¹

We talk to Wakan tanka and are sure he hears us and yet it is hard to explain what we believe about this. It is the general belief of the Indians that after a man dies his spirit is somewhere on the earth or in the sky; we do not know exactly where but we are sure that his spirit still lives. Sometimes people have agreed together that if it were possible for spirits to speak to men, they would make themselves known to their friends after they died, but they never came to speak to us again, unless, perhaps, in our sleeping dreams. So it is with Wakan tanka. We believe that he is everywhere, yet, he is to us as the spirits of our friends, whose voices we cannot hear.

MATO-KUWAPI/CHASED-BY-BEARS
(Santee-Yanktonai Sioux), circa 1918[42]

sun'kaa	wolf
mici'la	I considered myself
yun'kan	but
hinhan'	the owls
hoton'pi	are hooting
yun'kan	and
hanko'waki pelo'	the night I fear

GRAY HAWK (Teton Sioux),
translated in 1918[43]

The body dies. The body is just what the soul possesses or the soul was in. The soul lives on.

SUSIE BILLIE, age 102 (Seminole), 1993[44]

Man's life is transitory, and being so it is useless to harbor the fear of death, for death must come sooner or later to everybody; man and all living creatures come into existence, pass on, and are gone, while the mountains and rivers remain ever the same—these alone of all visible things abide unchanging.

Tenet of the Hethu'shka Society
(Omaha), translated in 1905[45]

The feeling of grandparents for their grandchildren can be expressed this way: "Our children are dear to us; but when we have grandchildren, they seem to be more dear than our children were." You might say that the grandmother falls all over herself to try to show her appreciation for her grandchild. It goes right back to those wishes that were made for them when they were little girls that they would live to be grandmothers someday. So when the time comes and they reach grandmotherhood they do extra little duties to show their appreciation.

HENRY OLD COYOTE (Crow), 1974[46]

Sung by Tatantka Iyotake (Sitting Bull) After Surrendering to the United States Authorities Following the Custer Fight

iki'cize	A warrior
waon'kon	I have been
wana'	now
hena'la yelo'	It is all over
iyo'tiye kiya'	a hard time
waon'	I have

SITTING BULL (Lakota), circa 1877[47]

When we examine American Indian tribal religion, we find a notable absence of the fear of death. Burial mounds indicate a belief that life after death was a continuation of the life already experienced. Personal possessions, familiar tools and weapons, cooking utensils and frequently food were placed near the body so that

49

it would be sustained in the next life. It was not contemplated that the soul would have to account for misdeeds and lapses from a previously established ethical norm. All of that concern was expressed while the individual was alive. Some tribes viewed entrance into the next life as almost a mechanical process to which everyone was subject, a natural cosmic process to which all things were bound. . . .

Some decades ago I attended a burial in a Christian cemetery at Mission, South Dakota. After the body was in the grave and the several mourners were standing at the grave, an old woman stepped forward and put an orange on the grave. The Episcopal priest who had conducted the service rushed over and took the orange away, saying "When do you think the departed will come and eat this orange?" One of the Sioux men standing there said, "When the soul comes to smell the flowers." No one said anything after that.

VINE DELORIA, JR. (Oglala Sioux), 1973[48]

chapter Fɪᴠᴇ

THE SKY ABOVE

YUCHI

Song of the Thunders

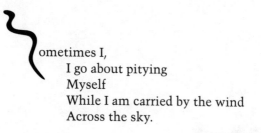

ometimes I,
    I go about pitying
    Myself
    While I am carried by the wind
    Across the sky.

ANONYMOUS
(Chippewa), translated in 1910[49]

It is above that
you and I shall go;
Along the Milky Way
You and I shall go
Along the flower trail
you and I shall go
Picking flowers on our way
You and I shall go.

ANONYMOUS (Wintu), translated in 1935[50]

We return thanks to the moon and stars, which give us light when the sun has gone to rest. We thank thee, that thy wisdom has so kindly provided, that light is never wanting to us. Continue unto us this goodness.

We return thanks to the sun, that he has looked upon the earth with beneficent eye. We thank thee, that thou hast, in thy unbounded wisdom, commanded the sun to regulate the return of the seasons, to dispense heat and cold, and to watch over the comfort of thy people. Give unto us that wisdom, which will guide us in the path of truth. Keep us from all evil ways, that the sun may never hide his face from us for shame and leave us in darkness.

From a traditional Thanksgiving address
spoken by SOSE-HA-WA (Seneca), translated
by HA-SA-NO-AN-DA/ELY PARKER, 1851[51]

Sing your song
        looking up
                at the sky.

Personal song of an old
blind woman (Nootka), translated in 1939[52]

A man may be able to do things in a mysterious way, but none has ever been found who could command the sun and moon or change the seasons. The most wonderful things which a man can do are different from the works of nature. When the seasons changed, we regarded it as a gift from the sun, which is the strongest of all the mysterious *wakan* powers. . . .

ANONYMOUS (Teton Sioux), circa 1918[53]

Birds have always been important to the Indian because they go where they wish, they light where they may, and they're free. We take these feathers from the birds. We use them in our ceremony because the feathers remind us of the Creator. The eagle flies highest in the sky of all the birds and so he is the nearest to the Creator, and his feather is the most sacred of all. He is the highest of the birds and so belongs to all the tribes, to all the peoples.

BUFFALO JIM (Seminole), 1990[54]

My father explained this to me. "All things in this world," he said, "have souls or spirits. The sky has a spirit, the clouds have spirits; the sun and moon have spirits; so have animals, trees, grass, water, stones, *everything.*"

EDWARD GOODBIRD (Hidatsa), 1914[55]

From The Song of the Stars

We are the stars which sing.
We sing with our light.
We are the birds of fire.
We fly over the sky.
Our light is a voice.
We make a road
For the spirit to pass over.

TRADITIONAL SONG (Passamaquoddy)

The Indian loved to worship. From birth to death he revered his surroundings. He considered himself born in the luxurious lap of Mother Earth and no place to him was humble. There was nothing between him and the Big Holy. The contact was immediate and personal and the blessings of Wakan Tanka flowed over the Indian like rain showered from the sky. Wakan Tanka was not aloof, apart, and ever seeking to quell evil forces. He did not punish the animals and the birds, and likewise He did not punish man. He was not a punishing God. For there was never a question as to the supremacy of an evil power over and above the power of Good. There was but one ruling power, and that was Good.

CHIEF LUTHER STANDING BEAR
(Lakota), 1933[56]

A wise elder among my people, the Tewa, frequently used the phrase *Pin pe obi*, "look to the mountaintop," when he was alive. I first heard it 25 years ago when I was seven years old, practicing for the first time to participate in relay races we run in the Pueblo country to give strength to the sun father as he journeys across the sky. I was at one end of the earth track which ran from east to west, like the path of the sun. The old man, who was blind, called me to him and said, "Young one, as you run look to the mountaintop," and he pointed to Tsikomo, the western sacred mountain of the Tewa world, which loomed off in the distance. "Keep your eyes fixed on that mountain and you will feel the miles melt beneath your feet. Do this and in time you will feel as if you can leap over bushes, trees, and even the river." I tried to understand what this last statement meant, but I was too young.

On another occasion, a few days later, I asked him if I could really learn to leap over the treetops. He smiled and said, "Whatever life's challenges you may face, remember always to look to the mountaintop, for in so doing you look to greatness. Remember this, and let no problem, no matter how great it may seem, discourage you, nor let anything less than the mountaintop distract you. This is the one thought I want to leave you with. And in that dim coming time when we shall meet again, it shall be on the mountaintop." I did not have long to wonder why, for the following month, when the cornstalks were sturdy on the land, he died quietly in his sleep, having seen eighty-seven summers.

ALFONSO ORTIZ (Tewa), 1973[57]

Song to the Pleiades

Look as they rise, rise
Over the line where sky meets the earth;
Pleiades!
Lo! They ascending, come to guide us,
Leading us safely, keeping us one;
Pleiades,
Teach us to be, like you, united.

TRADITIONAL (Pawnee), translated in 1904[58]

chapter six

THE
EARTH
BELOW

CHOCTAW

I t's really important for women to take care of the Mother Earth that we live on today. ... Your mother might die, but you still live on this earth. ... Your mother's the one that does everything for you. The Mother Earth does the same.

LENA SOOKTIS (Northern Cheyenne), 1993[59]

Every part of this soil is sacred in the estimation of my people. Every hillside, every valley, every plain and grove, has been made holy by some sad or happy event in days long vanished. Even the rocks, which seem to be voiceless and dead as they swelter in the sun along the silent shore, thrill with memories of stirring events connected with the lives of my people. And the very dust upon which you now stand responds more lovingly to their footsteps than to yours, because it is rich with the blood of our ancestors and our bare feet are conscious of the sympathetic touch.

CHIEF SEATHL (Duwamish-Suquamish), 1854[60]

My young men shall never work. Men who work cannot dream, and wisdom comes in dreams.

You ask me to plow the ground. Shall I take a knife and tear my mother's breast? Then when I die she will not take me to her bosom to rest.

You ask me to dig for stone. Shall I dig under her skin for bones? Then when I die I cannot enter her body to be born again.

You ask me to cut grass and make hay and sell it, and be rich like white men. But how dare I cut off my mother's hair?

SMOHALLA (Nez Perce), circa 1850[61]

We humans must come again to a moral comprehension of the earth and air. We must live according to the principle of a land ethic. The alternative is that we shall not live at all.

N. SCOTT MOMADAY (Kiowa), 1970[62]

The Great Spirit is our father, but the Earth is our mother. She nourishes us; that which we put into the ground she returns to us, and healing plants she gives us likewise. If we are wounded, we go to our mother and seek to lay the wounded part against her, to be healed.

BEDAGI (Wabanaki), circa 1900⁶³

The old people came literally to love the soil and they sat or reclined on the ground with a feeling of being close to a mothering power. It was good for the skin to touch the earth and the old people liked to remove their moccasins and walk with bare feet on the sacred earth. Their tipis were built upon the earth and their altars were made of earth. The birds that flew in the air came to rest upon the earth and it was the final abiding place of all things that lived and grew. The soil was soothing, strengthening, cleansing and healing.

That is why the old Indian still sits upon the earth instead of propping himself up away from its life-giving forces. For him, to sit or lie upon the ground is to be able to think more deeply and feel more keenly.

CHIEF LUTHER STANDING BEAR
(Lakota), 1933[64]

The soil you see is not ordinary soil—it is the dust of the blood, the flesh, and the bones of our ancestors. . . . You will have to dig down through the surface before you can find nature's earth, as the upper portion is Crow. The land, as it is, is my blood and my dead; it is consecrated; and I do not want to give up any portion of it.

CURLEY (Crow), 1936[65]

Words Spoken in Opposition to a Treaty Selling Land

I wonder if the ground has anything to say? I wonder if the ground is listening to what is said? I wonder if the ground would come alive and what is on it? Though I hear what the ground says. The ground says, It is the Great Spirit who placed me here. The Great Spirit tells me to take care of the Indians, to feed them aright. . . .

The same way the ground says, it was from me human beings were made. The Great Spirit, in placing human beings on the earth, desired them to take good care of the ground and to do each other no harm.

YOUNG CHIEF (Cayuse), 1855[66]

Wica'hcala kin   The old men
heya'pelo'   say
maka' kin   the earth
lece'la   only
tehan yunke'lo   endures
eha' pelo'   You spoke
ehan'kecon   truly
wica' yaka pelo'   You are right.

USED-AS-A-SHIELD (Teton Sioux),
translated in 1918[67]

In the Western Shoshone way a long time ago, when your mother got old, you didn't throw her away; you brought her into your home and took care of her. This is the way we are supposed to take care of the Earth, too. The same way we should take care of our mothers. It's basically just common sense.

CARRIE DANN (Western Shoshone), 1993[68]

Non-Native people have a tendency to want to fix everything. Sometimes things don't need to be fixed immediately. If you let nature take care of itself and heal itself, you will notice that it will do just that. Yellowstone Park is a good example. It experienced charring and burning, and within less than a year's time, people began to see regrowth and the news media was shocked. Nature does this all the time. We as human beings are part of the earth and a part of nature. Allow nature to heal and it will happen.

GAWANAHS/TONYA GONELLA FRICHNER
(Onondaga), 1993[69]

chapter seven

THE SACRED PLACE WITHIN

But if the vision was true and mighty, as I know, it is true and mighty yet; for such things are of the spirit, and it is in the darkness of their eyes that men get lost.

BLACK ELK (Oglala Lakota), 1931[70]

The smarter a man is
the more he needs God
to protect him from thinking
he knows everything.

GEORGE WEBB (Pima), 1959[71]

In the old days our people had no education. They could not learn from books or from teachers. All their wisdom and knowledge came to them in dreams. They tested their dreams, and in that way learned their own strength.

ANONYMOUS ELDER (Chippewa), 1929[72]

One of our old, old holy men said, "Every step you take on earth should be a prayer. The power of a pure and good soul is in every person's heart and will grow as a seed as you walk in a sacred manner. And if every step you take is a prayer, then you will always be walking in a sacred manner."

CHARMAINE WHITE FACE (Oglala Lakota), 1993[73]

Everything is laid out for you.
Your path is straight ahead of you.
Sometimes it's invisible but it's there.
You may not know where it's going,
but you have to follow that path.
It's the path to the Creator.
It's the only path there is.

CHIEF LEON SHENANDOAH (Onondaga), 1990[74]

The man who preserves his selfhood ever calm and unshaken by the storms of existence—not a leaf, as it were, astir on the tree; not a ripple upon the surface of the shining pool—his, in the mind of the unlettered sage, is the ideal attitude and conduct of life.

If you ask him: "What is silence?" he will answer: "It is the Great Mystery!" "The holy silence is His voice!" If you ask: "What are the fruits of silence?" he will say: "They are self-control, true courage or endurance, patience, dignity, and reverence. Silence is the corner-stone of character."

"Guard your tongue in youth," said the old chief, Wabashaw, "and in age you may mature a thought that will be of service to your people."

OHIYESA/DR. CHARLES A. EASTMAN
(Santee Dakota), 1902[75]

Sovereignty is something that goes in ever-widening circles, beginning with yourself. . . . If a person can go out into the stream and fish for their needs, if they can do whatever they have to do to provide for those who are dependent on them, then that person is sovereign. Sovereignty isn't something someone gives you. You can't give us our sovereignty. Sovereignty isn't a privilege someone gives you. It's a responsibility you carry inside yourself.

BAWDWAY WI DUN/
EDWARD BENTON-BENAI
(Ojibway), 1990[76]

I do not always ask, in my prayers and discussions, for only those things I would like to see happen, because no man can claim to know what is best for mankind. *Wakan-Tanka* and Grandfather alone know what is best, and this is why, even though I am worried, my attitude is not overcome with fear of the future. I submit always to *Wakan-Tanka*'s will. This is not easy, and most people find it impossible, but I have seen the power of prayer and I have seen God's desires fulfilled. So I pray always that God will give me wisdom to accept his way of doing things.

FRANK FOOLS CROW (Teton Sioux), 1979[77]

Hopi Ethics

Be happy in order to live long.
Worry makes you sick.

Getting mad is a bad habit.

If an innocent man doesn't get angry,
he'll live a long while.
A guilty man will get sick
because of bad thoughts.

Happiness is not only good in itself
but it is very healthful.

TRADITIONAL (Hopi), recorded in 1954[78]

ood medicine is for healing. To do it, a lot
of it is belief in it. If you don't believe in
something, if your heart's not in it, it'll be hard to
heal.

AGNES CYPRESS (Seminole), 1993[79]

There is no doubt that the Indian held medicine close to spiritual things, but in this also he has been much misunderstood; in fact, everything that he held sacred is indiscriminately called "medicine," in the sense of mystery or magic. As a doctor, he was originally very adroit and often successful. He employed only healing bark, roots and leaves with whose properties he was familiar, using them in the form of a distillation or tea and always singly. The stomach or internal bath was a valuable discovery of his, and the vapor or Turkish bath was in general use. He could set a broken bone with fair success, but never practiced surgery in any form. In addition to all this, the medicine man possessed much personal magnetism, and authority, and in his treatment often sought to reestablish the equilibrium of the patient through mental and spiritual influences—a sort of primitive psycho-therapy.

The Sioux word for the healing art is "wah-pee-yah," which literally means readjusting or making anew. "Pay-jee-hoo-tah," literally root, means medicine, and "wakan" signifies spirit or mystery. Thus the three ideas were carefully distinguished. It is important to remember that in the old days the "medicine-man" received no payment for his services, which were of the nature of an honorable function or office. When the idea of payment and barter was introduced among us, and valuable presents or fees began to be demanded for treating the sick, the ensuing greed and rivalry led to many demoralizing practices, and in time to the rise of the modern "conjurer," who is generally a fraud and trickster of the grossest kind. It is fortunate that his day is practically over.

OHIYESA/DR. CHARLES A. EASTMAN
(Santee Dakota), 1902[80]

People want to learn about spirituality so badly that they will follow anything that comes before them, but actually what they are doing is hurting themselves if they don't understand it. You have to be sincere whenever you're practicing the

Indian religion; it's too sacred a thing to mess around with.

People should go right down to their own roots and learn from there, learn from their own beginnings, and then get to where they have it within themselves.

OLIVIA POURIER, Black Elk's granddaughter
(Lakota), 1993[81]

Spoken by Red Jacket to a Missionary

You say that you are sent to instruct us how to worship the Great Spirit agreeably according to his mind, and if we do not take hold of the religion which you white people teach, we shall be unhappy hereafter. You say that you are right, and we are lost. How do we know this to be true?

We understand that your religion is written in a book. If it was intended for us as well as you, why has the Great Spirit not given it to us, and not only to us, but why did he not give to our forefathers the knowledge of that book with the means of understanding it rightly? We only know what you tell us about it; how shall we know when to believe, being so often deceived by the white people?

Brother, you say there is but one way to worship and serve the Great Spirit. If there is but one religion, why do you white people differ so much about it? Why do not all agree, as you can all read the book?

Brother, we do not understand these things. We are told that your religion was given to your forefathers, and has been handed down from father to son. We also have a religion which was given to our ancestors, and has been handed down to us their children. We worship that way. It teaches us to be thankful for all the favors we receive; to love each other, and to be united. We never quarrel about religion.

RED JACKET/SAGOYEWATHA (Seneca), 1805[82]

Spoken by a Hopi Elder to a Missionary

We may be foolish in the eyes of the white people, for we are a very simple people. We live close to our great mother, the Earth. We believe in our God as you believe in your God, but we believe that our God is best for us. Our God talks to us and tells us what to do. Our God gives us the rain cloud and the sunshine, the corn and all things to sustain life, and our God gave us these things before we ever heard of your God. If your God is so great, let him speak to me as my God speaks to me, in my heart and not from a white man's mouth. Your God is a cruel God and not all-powerful, for you always talk about a devil and a hell where people go after they die. Our God is all-powerful and all-good, and there is no devil and there is no hell in our Underworld where we go after we die. No, I would rather stick to my God and my religion than to change to yours, for there is more happiness in my religion than there is in yours.

ANONYMOUS (Hopi), 1907[83]

I'm the only one who's responsible for my soul, if I don't do the right thing here. I'm at fault, not him, not the church, not that mountain over there or the sun. This is the way they teach Indian religion. No one is going to influence you, no one is going to bring you up to your grave, but yourself.

ALEX SALUSKIN (Yakima), 1970[84]

Our people get tromped on, stepped on, and lied to—the whole works—but you can't dwell on pain. That is the past. With all of us working for a better tomorrow, things can get better. If we dwell on all the hurts, nothing will come of it except hard feelings. We have enough of those.

We have to work for a better tomorrow and for all the pain to heal in our spirits. Whenever something painful comes about, I believe in the Creator. He helps me to get over what is bothering me. He helps me to get over the hurt.

MILDRED KALAMA IKEBE
(Nisqually, Puyallup, Native Hawaiian), 1993[85]

his is what the spirit tells me—get my people together. Get them to believe because if you don't they are going to go wild. They are going to kill one another. Whoever has sacred places must wake them up, the same as I am doing here—to keep my old world within my heart and with the spiritual. For them to help me and for me to help my people.

FLORA JONES (Wintu), 1975[86]

I don't know where our humor comes from, but it can be the worst situation in the whole world and you can sit there and you can laugh. I guess it's just because the good inside of us always comes out no matter when or where it is.

RENNE HALLETT (Tonawanda Seneca), 1993[87]

The first peace, which is the most important, is that which comes within the souls of men when they realize their relationship, their oneness, with the universe and all its Powers, and when they realize that at the center of the universe dwells *Wakan-Tanka*, and that this center is really everywhere, it is within each of us. This is the real Peace, and the others are but reflections of this. The second peace is that which is between two individuals, and the third is that which is made between two nations. But above all you should understand that there can never be peace between nations until there is first known that true peace which, as I have often said, is within the souls of men.

BLACK ELK (Oglala Lakota), 1948[88]

chapter Eight

MIMBRES

THE CIRCLE

PIMA

Everything's a circle. We're each responsible for our own actions. It will come back.

BETTY LAVERDURE (Ojibway), 1993[89]

You have noticed that everything an Indian does is in a circle and that is because the Power of the World always works in circles and everything tries to be round. In the old days when we were a strong and happy people, all our power came to us from the sacred hoop of the nation, and so long as that hoop was unbroken, the people flourished. . . . Everything the Power of the World does is done in a circle. The sky is round and I have heard that the earth is round like a ball and so are all the stars. The wind, in its greatest power, whirls. Birds make their nests in circles, for theirs is the same religion as ours. The sun comes forth and goes down again in a circle. The moon does the same, and both are round.

Even the seasons form a great circle in their changing, and always come back again to where they were. The life of a man is a circle from childhood to childhood and so it is in everything where power moves.

BLACK ELK (Oglala Lakota), 1931[90]

It was the wind
that gave them life.
It is the wind
that comes out of our mouths
now that gives us life.
When this ceases to blow we die.
In the skin at the tips of our fingers
we see the trail of the wind;
it shows us the wind blew
when our ancestors were created.

ANONYMOUS (Navajo), 1897[91]

Plants are thought to be alive,
their juice is their blood, and they grow.

The same is true of trees.
All things die,
therefore all things have life.
Because all things have life,
gifts have to be given to all things.

WILLIAM RALGANAL BENSON
(Pomo), 1993[92]

ur prophecies tell of white people. They were once our brothers who went away to the East. They learned all about inventions there. They were supposed to come back here with the inventions and help us to a better life. They would complete our spiritual circle. But, instead of bringing the symbol of a circle, they brought the symbol of a cross. The circle brings people together, the cross sets them apart.

THOMAS BANYACA (Hopi), 1990[93]

When I was ten years of age I looked at the land and the rivers, the sky above, and the animals around me and could not fail to realize they were made by some great power. I was so anxious to understand this power that I questioned the trees and the bushes. It seemed as though the flowers were staring at me, and I wanted to ask them, "Who made you?" I looked at the moss-covered stones, some of them seemed to have the features of a man, but they could not answer me. Then I had a dream, and in my dream one of those small round stones appeared to me and told me that the maker of all was Wakan Tanka, and that in order to honor him I must honor his works in nature.

TATANKA-OHITIKA/BRAVE BUFFALO
(Teton Sioux), 1918[94]

One major difference between our people and those of the dominant society today is humility. Among our people, no matter how far or how high a person goes, they know they are small in the presence of God and universe.

LINCOLN TRITT
(Gwichin Athabascan), 1989[95]

We believe that the spirit pervades all creation and that every creature possesses a soul in some degree, though not necessarily a soul conscious of itself. The tree, the waterfall, the grizzly bear, each is an embodied Force, and as such an object of reverence.

OHIYESA/DR. CHARLES A. EASTMAN
(Santee Dakota), 1902[96]

We do not like to harm the trees. Whenever we can, we always make an offering of tobacco to the trees before we cut them down. We never waste the wood, but use all that we cut down. If we did not think of their feelings, and did not offer them tobacco before cutting them down, all the other trees in the forest would weep, and that would make our hearts sad, too.

ANONYMOUS (Mesquakie), 1939[97]

Hopi symbol for Mother Earth

All life is wakan. So also is everything which exhibits power, whether in action, as the winds and drifting clouds, or in passive endurance, as the boulder by the wayside. For even the commonest sticks and stones have a spiritual essence which must be reverenced as a manifestation of the all-pervading mysterious power that fills the universe.

FRANCIS LAFLESCHE (Osage), 1925[98]

Everything is together—spiritual and political—because when the Creator, whoever the Creator is, made this world, he touched the world all together and it automatically became spiritual. . . .

TOM PORTER (Mohawk), 1987[99]

Yuki Initiation Song

The rock did not come here by itself.
The tree does not stand here of itself.
There is one who made all of this,
Who shows us everything.

TRADITIONAL (Yuki), translated in 1925[100]

Listen to the air. You can hear it, feel it, smell it, taste it. Woniya wakan—the holy air—which renews all by its breath. Woniya, woniya wakan—spirit, life, breath, renewal—it means all that. Woniya—we sit together, don't touch, but something is there; we feel it between us, as a presence. A good way to start thinking about nature, talk about it. Rather talk to it, talk to the rivers, to the lakes, to the winds as our relatives.

JOHN LAME DEER
(Miniconjou Sioux), 1972[101]

In the beginning we were given our Instructions of how to live. So that's been handed down from generations to generations until now. "This is how to live."

We were told to be good to one another. Respect one another. Take care of each other, as well as ourself. These are some of our Instructions. As long as we do what we're supposed to do, these are the basic important things, then we have no problems. Once we start hating our neighbor and start stealing from our neighbor and start lying to them and not growing our food but depending on somebody else to grow the food, that's when we unbalance ourself. That's what the legends, our stories, tell us.

VICKIE DOWNEY (Tewa-Tesuque Pueblo), 1993[102]

The lands of the planet call to humankind for redemption. But it is a redemption of sanity, not a supernatural reclamation project at the end of history. The planet itself calls to the other living species for relief. Religion cannot be kept within the bounds of sermons and scriptures. It is a force in and of itself and it calls for the integration of lands and peoples in harmonious unity. The land waits for those who can discern their rhythms. The peculiar genius of each continent—each river valley, the rugged mountains, the placid lakes—all call for relief from the constant burden of exploitation.

VINE DELORIA, JR. (Lakota), 1973[103]

Know things in nature
are like a person.
Talk to tornados;
talk to the thunder.
They are your friends
and will protect you.

ANONYMOUS (Navajo), 1973[104]

From an Address Delivered to the
United Nations

Power is not manifested in the human being. True
power is in the Creator. If we continue to ignore the
message by which we exist and we continue to de-
stroy the source of our lives then our children will
suffer. . . . I must warn you that the Creator made
us all equal with one another. And not only human

beings, but all life is equal. The equality of our life is what you must understand and the principles by which you must continue on behalf of the future of this world. Economics and technology may assist you, but they will also destroy you if you do not use the principles of equality. Profit and loss will mean nothing to your future generations. . . .

I do not see a delegation for the four-footed. I see no seat for the eagles. We forget and we consider ourselves superior, but we are after all a mere part of the Creation. And we must continue to understand where we are. And we stand between the mountain and the ant, somewhere and there only, as part and parcel of the Creation. It is our responsibility, since we have been given the minds to take care of these things. The elements and the animals, and the birds, they live in a state of grace. They are absolute, they can do no wrong. It is only we, the two-leggeds, that can do this. And when we do this to our brothers, to our own brothers, then we do the worst in the eyes of the Creator.

OREN LYONS (Onondaga), 1977[105]

From a Yokuts Prayer

My words are tied in one
With the great mountains,
With the great rocks,
With the great trees,
In one with my body
And my heart.
Do you all help me
with supernatural power,
And you, day,
And you, night!
All of you see me
One with this world!

TRADITIONAL (Yokuts),
translated in 1925[106]

It's so sad when people try to homogenize every-
body. Everybody be the same. We're just like flow-

ers on the earth. [It] would be so boring when we go out there and we see nothing but daisies, black-and-white daisies. Different people, different ideas, and different beliefs, makes life so much more interesting.

CECILIA MITCHELL (Mohawk), 1993[107]

There need be no trouble.
Treat all men alike.
Give them all the same law.
Give them all an even chance
to live and grow.
All men were made
by the same Great Spirit Chief.
They are all brothers.
The earth is the mother of all people
and all people should have equal rights upon it.

CHIEF JOSEPH (Nez Perce), 1879[108]

Notes

1. From "The Dine: Origin Myths of the Navajo Indians," by Aileen O'Bryan, *Bureau of American Ethnology Bulletin* 163 (1956).

2. Reprinted from *Black Elk Speaks*, by John G. Neihardt, by permission of the Univ. of Nebraska Press. Copyright 1932, 1959, 1972, by John G. Neihardt. Copyright © 1961 by the John G. Neihardt Trust.

3. and 4. Copyright © 1990 by Harvey Arden and Steve Wall, from *Wisdomkeepers*, Beyond Words Publishing, Inc., Hillsboro, OR.

5. From "Night Chant, A Navajo Ceremony," translated by Washington Matthews, *American Museum of Natural History Memoirs*, 6 (New York, 1902), and *Memoirs of the American Folk-Lore Society*, 5 (Boston: Houghton & Mifflin, 1897).

6. From *Indian Heritage, Indian Pride*, by Jimalee Burton (Norman: Univ. of Oklahoma Press, 1974), 55. Reprinted by permission.

7. From *Indian Roots of American Democracy*, edited by José Barriero (Ithaca, NY: Akwe:kon Press, 1992).

8. From "An Indian's View of Indian Affairs," by Chief Joseph, *North American Review* 127 (April 1879).

9. From *Wisdom's Daughters: Conversations with Women Elders of Native America*, by Steve Wall. Copyright © 1993 by Steve Wall. Reprinted by permission of HarperCollins Publishers, Inc.

10. Words spoken in 1609 and recorded by John Smith, from *Lives of Celebrated American Indians*, by Samuel Griswold Goodrich (Boston: Bradbury, Sooden, 1843).

11. From *Lahontan's New Voyages to North America*, by Rueben Gold Thwaites (Chicago, 1905).

12. From *New Relations of Gaspeia, with the Customs and Religion of the Gaspeian Indians,* by Father Christian LeClercq, translated by William F. Ganong (Toronto: Champlain Society, 1910).

13. From "Mu'ndu Wi'Go: Mohegan Poems," by Joseph Bruchac, *Blue Cloud Quarterly* (1978); translated from "A Mohegan Pequot Diary," recorded by Frank Speck, *Bureau of American Ethnology Bulletin* 43 (1925).

14. From *The Law of the Great Peace* (White Roots of Peace, no date); may be ordered from Mohawk Nation, Rooseveltown, NY 13683.

15. From "Zuni Origin Myths," by Ruth L. Bunzel, *Bureau of American Ethnology Bulletin* 47 (1929–30).

16. From "Handbook of the Indians of California," by Theodore Kroeber, *Bureau of American Ethnology Bulletin* 79 (1925).

17. From *The Sacred: Ways of Knowledge, Sources of Life,* by Peggy Beck, Anna Lee Walters, and Nia Francisco (Tsaile, AZ: Navajo Community College Press, 1992), 49. Used by permission.

18. Reprinted from *Land of the Spotted Eagle,* by Luther Standing Bear, by permission of the Univ. of Nebraska Press. Copyright © 1933 by Luther Standing Bear. Renewal copyright © 1960 by May Jones.

19. From *Teachings from the American Earth,* by Barbara and Dennis Tedlock (New York: Liveright Publishing, 1975). Copyright © 1975 by Barbara and Dennis Tedlock.

20. From *The Good Message of Handsome Lake,* by Joseph Bruchac (Greensboro, NC: Unicorn Press, 1979), adapted from "The Gai'wio (The Good Message)."

21. From "Chippewa Customs," by Frances Densmore, *Bureau of American Ethnology Bulletin* 86 (1929).

22. From "The Winnebago Tribe," by Paul Radin, *Bureau of American Ethnology Bulletin* 37 (1923).

23. Excerpt from *Plenty-Coups, Chief of the Crows* by Frank B. Linderman. Copyright © 1930 by Frank B. Linderman. Renewal copyright © 1957 by Norma Linderman Waller, Verne Linderman, and Wilda Linderman. Reprinted by permission of HarperCollins Publishers, Inc.

24. Copyright © 1990 by Harvey Arden and Steve Wall, from *Wisdomkeepers*, Beyond Words Publishing, Inc., Hillsboro, OR.

25. From *Civilization*, by Thomas Wildcat Alford, as told to Florence Drake (Norman: Univ. of Oklahoma Press, 1936).

26. From a speech given at a United Nations Conference in Geneva, Switzerland, September 1977; published in *Akwesasne Notes* (December 1977), 11.

27. From *Women of the Native Struggle* by Ronnie Farley. Copyright © 1993 by Ronnie Farley. Reprinted by permission of Crown Publishers, Inc.

28. From "The Social Organization of the Western Apache," by Grenville Goodwin, *University of Chicago Publications in Anthropology, Ethnology Series* (Chicago: Univ. of Chicago Press, 1942), 258.

29. From "Ethnology of the Kwakiutl," by Franz Boas, *Bureau of American Ethnology Bulletin* 35 (1921).

30. Excerpted from *Respect for Life*, edited by Sylvester M. Morey and Olivia Gilliam, 1974. Copyright © 1974 by The Myrin Institute, New York.

31. From *History of the Ojibway Indians*, by Chief Kahkewaquonaby/Peter Jones (London, 1861).

32. From "An Indian Chief," by Frances Garrecht, *Washington Historical Quarterly* 19 (July 1928).

33. Permission to reprint from *Cante ohitika Win (Brave-hearted Women): Images of Lakota Women from the Pine Ridge Reservation, South Dakota* by Carolyn Reyer granted by the Univ. of South Dakota Press, Vermillion, SD.

34. From Densmore, "Chippewa Customs."

35. From "Navajo Legends," translated by Washington Matthews, *Memoirs of the American Folk-Lore Society* 5 (Boston: Houghton & Mifflin, 1897).

36. From Farley, *Women of the Native Struggle*. Copyright © 1993 by Ronnie Farley. Reprinted by permission of Crown Publishers, Inc.

37. From "An Indian Soliloquy," by B. W. Aginsky, *American Journal of Sociology* 46 (1944).

38. From *Night Flying Woman: An Ojibway Narrative*, by Ignatia Broker (St. Paul: Minnesota Historical Society Press, 1983), 8. Reprinted by permission.

39. From Bruchac, *The Good Message of Handsome Lake*.

40. From *Canadian Portraits: Brant, Crowfoot, Oronhyatkha, Famous Indians*, by Ethel Brant Monture (Toronto: Irwin, 1960).

41. Excerpt from *Two Leggings: The Making of a Crow Warrior*, by Peter Nabokov. Copyright © 1967 by Peter Nabokov. Reprinted by permission of HarperCollins Publishers, Inc.

42. From "Teton Sioux Music," by Frances Densmore, *Bureau of American Ethnology Bulletin* 61 (1918).

43. From Densmore, "Teton Sioux Music."

44. From Wall, *Wisdom's Daughters*. Copyright © 1993 by Steve Wall. Reprinted by permission of HarperCollins Publishers, Inc.

45. From "The Omaha Tribe," by Alice C. Fletcher and Francis LaFlesche, *Bureau of American Ethnology 27th Annual Report* (1905–06).

46. Excerpted from *Respect for Life,* edited by Sylvester M. Morey and Olivia L. Gilliam, 1974. Copyright © 1974 by The Myrin Institute, New York.

47. From Densmore, "Teton Sioux Music."

48. From *God Is Red* by Vine Deloria, Jr., copyright © 1992; Fulcrum Publishing, 350 Indiana St., #350, Golden, CO 80401; 800-992-2908.

49. From Densmore, "Chippewa Music."

50. From "Wintu Songs," translated by D. Demetracopoulou, *Anthropos* 30 (1935), 487.

51. From *League of the Ho-de-no-sau-nee, or Iroquois,* by Lewis Henry Morgan (Rochester, 1851).

52. From "Nootka and Quileute Music," by Frances Densmore, *Bureau of American Ethnology Bulletin* 124 (1939).

53. From Densmore, "Teton Sioux Music."

54. Copyright © 1990 by Harvey Arden and Steve Wall, from *Wisdomkeepers,* Beyond Words Publishing, Inc., Hillsboro, OR.

55. From *Goodbird, the Indian* (1914; reprint, St. Paul: Minnesota Historical Society Press, 1985).

56. Reprinted from *Land of the Spotted Eagle,* by Luther Standing Bear, by permission of the Univ. of Nebraska Press. Copyright © 1933 by Luther Standing Bear. Renewal copyright © 1960 by May Jones.

57. From "Look to the Mountaintop," in *Essays on Reflection,* edited by E. Graham Ward (Boston: Houghton-Mifflin, 1973). Reprinted by permission of Alfonso Ortiz.

58. From "The Hako: A Pawnee Ceremony," by Alice C. Fletcher, *Bureau of American Ethnology 22nd Annual Report*, pt. 2 (1904).

59. From Wall, *Wisdom's Daughters*. Copyright © 1993 by Steve Wall. Reprinted by permission of HarperCollins Publishers, Inc.

60. From *The Washington Historical Society Quarterly* 22, no. 4 (October 1931).

61. From "The Nez Perce Indians," by Herbert J. Spinden, *American Anthropological Association Memoirs*, vol. 2, pt. 3 (1908).

62. From "The Man Made of Words," in *Indian Voices* (Berkeley: Indian Historian Press, 1970). Reprinted by permission.

63. From *The Indians' Book: Songs and Legends of the American Indian*, edited by Natalie Curtis (New York, 1907).

64. Reprinted from *Land of the Spotted Eagle* by Luther Standing Bear, by permission of the Univ. of Nebraska Press. Copyright © 1933 by Luther Standing Bear. Renewal copyright © 1960 by May Jones.

65. From *The Gospel of the Red Man*, by Ernest Thompson Seton (New York: Doubleday, 1936), 58–59.

66. From *The Indian Council in the Valley of the Walla Walla*, by Lawrence Kip (1855).

67. From Densmore, "Teton Sioux Music."

68. and 69. From Farley, *Women of the Native Struggle*. Copyright © 1993 by Ronnie Farley. Reprinted by permission of Crown Publishers, Inc.

70. Reprinted from *Black Elk Speaks*, by John G. Neihardt, by permission of the Univ. of Nebraska Press. Copyright © 1932, 1959, 1972, by John G. Neihardt. Copyright © 1961 by the John G. Neihardt Trust.

71. From *A Pima Remembers*, by George Webb, copyright © 1959. Used by permission of the Univ. of Arizona Press.

72. From Densmore, "Chippewa Customs."

73. From Farley, *Women of the Native Struggle*. Copyright © 1993 by Ronnie Farley. Reprinted by permission of Crown Publishers, Inc.

74. Copyright © 1990 by Harvey Arden and Steve Wall, from *Wisdomkeepers*, Beyond Words Publishing, Inc., Hillsboro, OR.

75. From *The Soul of the Indian, an Interpretation*, by Ohiyesa/Dr. Charles A. Eastman (Boston: McClure, Phillips, 1902).

76. Copyright © 1990 by Harvey Arden and Steve Wall, from *Wisdomkeepers*, Beyond Words Publishing, Inc., Hillsboro, OR.

77. From *Fools Crow*, by Thomas E. Mails (New York: Avon Books, 1979), 184.

78. Reprinted by permission of the Univ. of Chicago Press from *Hopi Ethics*, by Richard S. Brandt. Copyright © 1954 by Richard S. Brandt.

79. From Wall, *Wisdom's Daughters*. Copyright © 1993 by Steve Wall. Reprinted by permission of HarperCollins Publishers, Inc.

80. From Eastman, *The Soul of the Indian*.

81. From Farley, *Women of the Native Struggle*. Copyright © 1993 by Ronnie Farley. Reprinted by permission of Crown Publishers, Inc.

82. First recorded in 1811 by James D. Bemis, published many times subsequently, including in William F. Stone's *Life and Times of Sa-Go-Ye-Wat-Ha, or Red Jacket* (New York: Wiley & Putnam, 1841).

83. From "Festivals of the Hopi: Religion, the Inspiration, and Dancing, an Expression of Their National Ceremonies," *The Craftsmen*, 12 (1907).

84. Excerpted from *Seeking Life*, by Sylvester Morey, 1970. Copyright © 1970 by The Myrin Institute, New York.

85. From Farley, *Women of the Native Struggle*. Copyright © 1993 by Ronnie Farley. Reprinted by permission of Crown Publishers, Inc.

86. From "Flora, Shaman of the Wintu," by Peter M. Knudtson. With permission from *Natural History* (May 1975). Copyright © 1975 by The American Museum of Natural History.

87. From Wall, *Wisdom's Daughters*. Copyright © 1993 by Steve Wall. Reprinted by permission of HarperCollins Publishers, Inc.

88. From *The Sacred Pipe: Black Elk's Account of the Seven Rites of the Oglala Sioux*, recorded and edited by Joseph Epes Brown (Norman: Univ. of Oklahoma Press, 1953), 115. Reprinted by permission.

89. From Wall, *Wisdom's Daughters*. Copyright © 1993 by Steve Wall. Reprinted by permission of HarperCollins Publishers, Inc.

90. Reprinted from *Black Elk Speaks*, by John G. Neihardt, by permission of the Univ. of Nebraska Press. Copyright © 1932, 1959, 1972, by John G. Neihardt. Copyright © 1961 by the John G. Neihardt Trust.

91. From Matthews, "Navajo Legends."

92. From *The Way We Lived: California Indian Stories, Songs and Reminiscences*, edited by Malcolm Margolin, revised edition (Berkeley: Heyday Books, 1993), 87. Used by permission.

93. Copyright © 1990 by Harvey Arden and Steve Wall, from *Wisdomkeepers*, Beyond Words Publishing, Inc., Hillsboro, OR.

94. From Densmore, "Teton Sioux Music."

95. From *Raven Tells Stories*, edited by Joseph Bruchac (Greenfield Center, NY: Greenfield Review Press, 1991). Used by permission.

96. From Eastman, *The Soul of the Indian.*

97. From "Ethnology of the Fox Indians," by William Jones, *Bureau of American Ethnology Bulletin* 125 (1939).

98. From "The Osage Tribe, Rite of Vigil," *39th Annual Report of the Bureau of American Ethnology* (1925).

99. Excerpted from *Indian Roots of American Democracy*, edited by José Barriero (Ithaca, NY: Akwe:kon Press, 1992).

100. From *Handbook of the Indians of California*, by Arthur Kroeber (Washington, DC: U.S. Government Printing Office, 1925).

101. Copyright © 1972 by John Fire/Lame Deer and Richard Erdoes. Reprinted by permission of Simon & Schuster, Inc.

102. From Wall, *Wisdom's Daughters*. Copyright © 1993 by Steve Wall. Reprinted by permission of HarperCollins Publishers, Inc.

103. From *God Is Red* by Vine Deloria, Jr., copyright © 1992; Fulcrum Publishing, 350 Indiana St., #350, Golden, CO 80401; 800-992-2908.

104. From *Navajo Code Talkers*, by Doris A. Paul, Dorrance Publishing Co., Inc., Pittsburgh, 1973.

105. From a speech given at a United Nations Conference in Geneva, Switzerland, September 1977; published in *Akwesasne Notes* (December 1977), 7–8.

106. From *Handbook of the Indians of California*, by Arthur Kroeber (Washington, DC: U.S. Government Printing Office, 1925).

107. From Wall, *Wisdom's Daughters*. Copyright © 1993 by Steve Wall. Reprinted by permission of HarperCollins Publishers, Inc.

108. From "An Indian's View of Indian Affairs," by Chief Joseph, *North American Review* 127 (April 1879).